Where it all bega

My first born. I was 4 days early and I laid down on the brand new, grey sofa, in our brand new house, with our brand new cream carpets for a well deserved nap. Around 10:30, I was rudely awoken by sheer panic as I thought, "There's something coming out of me…" Somehow, I managed to waddle, at an impressive pace, to the toilet before Niagara Falls gushed from my gusset.
Honestly, it was like how they break in a comedy film. A literal bucketload. Each time it slowed to a trickle and I attempted to stand, another bucket was deployed.
Alone in the house, excitement and anxiety rushing through me, I became very aware that not only had I left my phone on the sofa, but the builders were working on the road immediately outside the living room window and as I'd basically pissed my pants, I had none on.
Thankfully, we'd had a leak from the toilet sink and there were still towels close by.
I covered my failing dignity, and fled through the house, grabbing my phone, dodging the workmen and headed into the safety of the shower where I made a few phone calls.

Half an hour later, as I remained half naked, dribbling into the shower, the curtains were delivered… I need them, there's potential I'll be in hospital for a while. I rolled a towel like a huge tampon and placed it between my legs and rushed to meet the delivery lady before she disappeared. Cue awkward "Oh, you're not starting are you?" conversation.
Actually, yes I am. But my partner is on his way, the hospital have been informed, I'm not in any pain and I know you're just being polite but please, just give me the curtains and let me go back inside…

This tap did not stop.
I'm just waddling about leaking everywhere.

And of course, I've not changed my address at the hospital yet, which feels like something that can't wait as I create a pool of amniotic fluid at your reception desk.
Finally in, water break confirmed, which would be pretty concerning at this point if I had actually just been pissing everywhere for a solid 4 hours but we're back home as I don't have any contractions.

So, I spend the evening over analysing every single twinge, movement, kick or lack of kicks, bouncing on a large, pink exercise ball, rearranging a towel tampon every 10 minutes to find a drier patch as my freedom dripped slowly from my vagina.

Somehow, I managed to sleep. To be fair, I can sleep on a galloping hedgehog so that's not a surprise really. We woke around 6am and went for a walk. We were new in the area and had a rough idea where the local shop was and I fancied a Lucozade. It was a 5 minute walk away, which took my fat ass 20. We had the same conversation 4 times with each dog walker we passed. And we made it to the shop then back home.

I decided, because a bath is the answer to everything apparently, that I would have a soak and see if I could speed things up a little however as I wanted to wash my hair, I nipped in the shower first. Hair clean, I attempted egress when I was shot in the stomach. Or at least that's how it felt.

Being a first time mum, I had apps galore on hand ready for me to start timing contractions, it was a fear of mine to attend hospital too early on in labour and be sent back home, but the pain didn't ebb and flow, it was constant. And not unbearable. So, I wasn't sure.

I'm on all fours at the top of the stairs shouting the love of my life, who is about to become a father, and knowing that the birthing process has technically already begun when my waters broke the day before, he's immediately on hand to ignore me for a good 10 minutes as he played on the X-Box, too loudly, so he couldn't hear my cries.

Eventually, when his character dies, he heeds the not so distant wailing of his damsel in distress and comes to investigate. He stares at me for a while as we try to establish if this is labour, if I can time the contractions, if it's time to go in. We decide to call the hospital. They decide not to answer 38 times. So, we get me dressed and downstairs. I wasn't lucky enough to hide from the workmen on this occasion who caught me at one of my high points, on all fours at the bottom of the stairs vomiting into a bin bag. The look of terror on their faces nothing compared to what would have been on mine should I have got orange Lucozade spew on the new carpets.

We make it into the car. And the carpets have survived. Then, to continue our lucky streak, we get through to the hospital. Now as I've explained, this pain although constant and very much uncomfortable, was not unbearable. I could talk through it. So the staff didn't believe me. I heard the disappointment in the lady's voice as I said we were en route as we'd struggled to get through for so long. She audibly sighed. I'm a bit of a machine love, I aint no hypochondriac. Anyway, we got there, and of course there's nowhere to park. This is when Our Lass starts to panic. Mate, we're here, calm down, could be a lot worse. He speaks to the happy fellow we see merrily popping parking tickets on the cars of monsters who are either sick or caring for the sick and after explaining the circumstances, we're granted permission to dump the car in the no parking zone until we can come back and move it later.

All I can think when in the lift is, "Don't be that knob head on your hands and knees, wailing." That is, that was all I could think until the emergent urge to vomit arose. We get to the tirage ward, I ring the bell, they ask my name and I inform them, "I'm going to be sick." They rush me to the toilet, a flurry of activity behind me as someone shouts, "Get a wheelchair!" I'm whisked straight through to the labour ward. Who's overreacting now eh?

They threw me in a room and I instantly needed to be naked.
The strangest sensation. I couldn't have anything touching my skin.
Which was unfortunate for Our Lass after the only advice he'd been given was to rub my back.
Do not touch me!
Put your hands to better use and close the blinds eh? We're only on the second floor and I'm in the niff here...

Shot of Pethidine and a nap later. I wake up with the urge to push.
It's not like on the TV is it?
They make it look like it's one push, head out, next one, baby out.
It comes and goes. Awful feeling really.

Anyway, I stood up, in the nud at the end of the bed, like a cow, with some kid I've not met playing Peekaboo from my nether regions. I'll not talk about shitting myself. No one needs to hear that.
Next thing I know, I'm being asked if a paramedic can come in and observe for training purposes. I oblige. He takes the best spot in the house and sits on the floor behind me with a bird's eye view of the show. It's not like I have any dignity left at this point anyway.

Not long after, I give birth. And it's a boy. I have a son.
A strange feeling, it's hard to feel joyous when you're stood naked in a room full of strangers.
They asked Our Lass if he'd like to cut the cord.
At this point, we realised the paramedic had the same name. Sit down son, she meant his dad.
The beautiful moment when father releases child into the world from the ties of his umbilical cord. Which is still attached to me by the way. And I'm still stood up so it's pretty taught already.
Cheers pal. Almost turned me inside out there.

Mother and baby safe and tucked up in bed.

Daddy decides to return to the car and get the suitcase full of all the things necessary for labour.
He gets a slight shock on his return as apparently, I retain placentas and was bleeding out on the bed. He says it was like walking into a horror scene. He looked at me, his face as white as mine from the blood loss and asked what the hell they'd done to me.

The midwife told me this was an important placenta.
I know that mate, it's inside me.
I'd had students in with me and I was the student midwife's 40th delivery. She needed 40 to be signed of as a fully-fledged, big girl midwife. However, it only counts if they deliver placenta too.
Fail. Oh God they tried but no. After a natural birth, I had to be whisked into theatre for placenta removal. Which required a spinal block, and a procedure you could do without after a human has just vacated your body. Champion.

Daddy, here's your son, I'll be back in a bit!

***

All that drama, and my first born, my beautiful, loving, kind, son.
Grows up calling me Debbie.
Debbie.
That's not even my name.

***

My second born. Ha. Buckle up for this one…

People told me that the second comes sooner as your body has done it all before.
Bull shit.
We decided to create a playmate for our beautiful Bill.
I loved pregnancy the first time. It was so magical and precious. A luxury that no longer exists when you have a toddler in tow. Second

pregnancy. Hated it. Put 4.5 stone on, again. Spent each day even more exhausted than usual. Couldn't nap whenever I wanted. Had to lug a kid around with me everywhere. Elephant ankles, brittle hips and a glass back. As I neared the end, the promise of not going overdue as it was my second turned only into torture.

On my due date, I went for a sweep.
The midwife going on and on about how she didn't understand why one had been authorised as it was my second and the risk of cord prolapse blah blah. I know she was just trying not to get my hopes up and I'm quite an understanding person. I explained that I understood and assured her I knew the baby was engaged as I couldn't walk, my hips were in agony and begged her to just look and see. She begrudgingly obliged. Curiously, she asked if I'd had any pains. I had not.
I was 5cm dilated.
5cm dilated.
I cried.
Today is the day! This turmoil is finally over!
Or is it?

Every night I went to bed thinking, this is the night.
And every morning I saw Our Lass go off to work thinking, today is the day.
(Our Lass has decided I tick over at 5cm dilated.)

5 days later...

I woke up just after 8am and thought, ooooo...
Some sort of twinge. Left it. Then again, like a period pain. Left it.
Then again. Hmmm.
I think today is the day.
I told Our Lass, he said he'd take the young 'un to Grandma's. I told him not to leave this house and to get him picked up. Roger that.

As Our Lass went to wake Bill, I attempted to get to the spare room to grab the only things that fit me that I'd set aside to wear to the hospital. I couldn't even get to the next room.
I'm stood on the landing, clinging onto the banister for dear life in the most excruciating pain I've ever experienced. The kind that makes you shake because you don't know whether to stand up, sit down, curl into a ball or spontaneously combust.

Bill, my little darling, sat at the top of the stairs on his Batmobile staring at me, "Debbie?" he asked worriedly.
"Debbie is fine, let's get dressed." Said his dad.

I phoned the hospital. Thank the Lord they answered first time. And this time I understood the talking thing as I forced out "Hang on a minute" painfully as I struggled to form words through the peak of a contraction. They calmly asked me to come in.

I had an urgent need to piss.
Got to the en-suite and my waters went. (I'm great at missing the carpet.)
I remember looking down and seeing one spot of blood.
Our Lass came in the bathroom and I told him I was bleeding.
"It's coming."
He thought I was just panicking, until he had a look and could see the head crowning.
One push later, he's now only 39 deliveries away from being a qualified midwife.

It's a boy.
08:20.

Bill, bezzing around our bedroom on his Batmobile saying, "Baby, it's a bit red."

When I finally got to hospital, baby already in arms, my midwife was the student I had with Bill.

Two babies I've had, and she's not delivered either of them.

Two ambulances, another trip into theatre, two blood transfusions, a week in hospital and 6 weeks injecting myself later. That was the entrance of Baby Tom.

Obviously named after Thomas Crapper, since he was born on one.

***

These are some of the things I've experienced in my journey into motherhood so far.

***

The expert use of swaddling and swaying to trick your baby into going to sleep for 15 minutes so that you can eat a bowl of disgustingly overcooked pasta for your breakfast at 14:30 whilst listening to a hypnotic loop of lullabies basically sums up motherhood.

***

When your baby has watched you spend the entire day rage cleaning the whole house and then shits in the bath.

***

How to wean a baby:

- Spend hours prepping and steaming veg before making them into purées and storing in tiny, little containers.
- Pick yours and baby's least stressful/tired time of day and gather at the dining table.

- Take a spoon and smear veg purée all over baby's face, head and clothing, making sure to get some up both of your noses and on the surrounding wall and floor areas.
- Attempt to wipe purée from baby's face, regularly tapping off the excess in the pot in order to clean the spoon.
- Realise that the pot is slowly filling up with saliva. Mix into the purée.
- Wait for baby to start blowing raspberries with a mouthful of food.
- Pretend they've actually consumed a worthy amount of food and give in.

How to feed a toddler:

- Discuss with them all the healthy options available and let them choose what they want.
- Prepare the agreed meal and present it in their preferred way considering the plate it's on and the shapes it's cut into.
- Wait for toddler to refuse the meal and cry as you explain that it's exactly what they asked for.
- Firmly stand your ground as you inform the toddler that this is what they asked for and that this is what they will be having.
- Make some jam on toast.
- Reward toddler with a treat for eating said jam on toast.

***

Anyone else panic when their baby wakes up screaming uncharacteristically?
Like, what in the name of Christ is happening? Cuddles not working, rocking a waste of energy... How fast is considered shaking the baby? Dummy lying dormant in a wide, screeching mouth. Here kid, have a bottle I know you don't want. Dose of Calpol anyone? Okay. Gripe water! Where's the bloody gripe water we've never opened? Wine? Whiskey? Benzodiazepines? Therapist? What do you want??

***

I've been smacked, had a spanner thrown at my head, been punched in the throat and been pissed on. Bill chose not to nap, has had numerous inexplicable meltdowns and has also peed on both sofas. To top the day off, he then shit on the carpet. Now I've mentioned bedtime, the manipulative little so and so wants to cuddle, and he can, because it makes it all worthwhile. Daddy, I owe you a replacement for the replacement wine I'm about to consume.

***

Gave Baby Tom his tea, offered him some water before his yoghurt as a palette cleanser.

10 minutes later

Bill: "Ah, where's the palette cleanser gone?"

***

So, my kid just pissed in my face. How's your day going?

***

The shit you deal with as a parent though. And I mean the literal shit. The baby one shits at least 3 times a day - which I'm sure is intentional to wind me up. And the toddler saves it all up to go once a week. That way, it's an all day job and stinks for the rest of the week...
On the way to the gym, put my hair behind my ears, can still smell it on my hands.
Thank God for alcohol gel.

***

I'm trying to teach the kids that they shouldn't talk to me until I've had a coffee in the morning, but Baby Tom doesn't yet understand "Don't roll in that sick!" So, it's not working out too well at the minute.

***

There's nothing quite like gazing in awe at the beauty you've created whilst watching your child sleep.
Until it wakes up and you're fuming because you had a list as long as Mr Tickle's arm of jobs to do whilst he napped and all you've done is watch Netflix.

***

One of the stupidest questions ever to be asked as a parent -

"Ah, is he teething?"

Well... he currently has no teeth and will have 20 by the time he's 2/3, each taking months to come through. So yeah, I'd say he's teething you fucking genius.

***

Just found a wet patch on my leg and I honestly don't know what it is. Hopefully it's sink water from washing the bottles, but it definitely could be piss. Or sick.

***

Having two kids is easy providing you don't want to eat or shower and that you have nothing to do and nowhere to go.

***

So earlier I had a decision to make... I could either:
a) Venture to the shop in a torrential downpour with both kids and the pram.
b) Stay at home safe and dry in existential crisis with no food, milk, coffee or will to live.

Either way the kids would be perfectly fine and it would be only I suffering unmentionably.

I chose A.
Mainly because I was unable to make a coffee, but also because 'hanger' is real and I didn't fancy having to eat puréed turkey and

garden pea pie to stop the teacher who lives next door from calling social services due to me screaming at the kids.

So off we went, Baby Tom dry as a bone without a care in the world, Bill having a blast jumping in every single puddle he saw, each of which resembling a small lake, shouting with excitement "Look Mummy, mud!!" And me, with rain in my eyes, soaked to the bone, looking like a drowned rat (particularly due to my rodent like features).

Now it's only a short walk. But it can take a good 15-20 minutes each way walking at toddler pace and trying to rush was counterproductive due to Bill then thinking I was leaving him behind and standing, crying, refusing to move for a short while.

Of course, now I've stopped the pram, Baby Tom realises he's hungry and starts crying also. I'm not sure if I'm crying too at this point, could just be rain.

We get to the shop, buy the essentials and get ready for the adventure home. Everyone's stood under the shelter outside the supermarket hoping the rain will ease so they don't have to step out in it, to travel 200 yards, with no children, to their cars... poor them.

It thunders. I look at Bill. I'm not sure if he's really experienced it before and he looks at me unsure too. I reassure him before we set off that it's just clouds crashing together because they're angry like mummy. I realise this perhaps isn't the best explanation. So, I tell him it's just Thor with his hammer.
Then it lightens and he asks if that's the Flash? Of course it is mate!

Screw it, we're already drenched. We leg it all the way home with Thor and the Flash like the absolute superheroes that we are. It wasn't that bad. And now, at least I have coffee.

***

Anyone ever met a baby that didn't like Spag Bol?

***

When the SMP finally ends:

I'm rich!! See you later Statutory Maternity Pay, you shit bitch!

pays bills

Oh...

***

I recently reinstated the window cleaner after having to cancel whilst on maternity pay.

I got so excited about the prospect of actually being able to see through the windows again that I forgot how painfully awkward it is when they come.

They came today. Just as I was getting ready to leave for our usual exciting trip to the shop. Even more exciting today as we were going via the Post Office.

So, this time, I thought great! I'll just pay them on the way out and leave them to it.
There was no pretending to 'act natural' as I cleaned, no wondering whether to change the channel when they approached the window halfway through a mucky scene in Sex and The City, and no hiding on the landing where there's no windows until they're done because I've just got out of the shower.

Bill however, had a different plan.

He didn't want to go to the shops. He didn't want to get his shoes on. He basically didn't want to do anything I'd asked of him and decided to kick off royally.

So today, the window cleaners got their best show yet. A war of wills between mother and child with a soundtrack of screaming all round.
Bill screaming in an unjust rage, me screaming for mercy and Baby Tom screaming for being left unoccupied waiting for us in the pram.

I could see the pain in their awkward smiles as I pretended not to look at them and they pretended not to have witnessed the entire ordeal.

***

My first child -
My mother: "Is he alright with that?"
Me: "He's nearly 1, a chip isn't going to hurt him."

My second child -
My mother: "Just nipping to McDonalds, shall I get Baby Tom a burger?"
Me: "He's 9 month old mother, no!"

***

Throwback to being overdue:

If anyone has a voodoo doll of me could they dilate its cervix.
Thanks in advance.

***

As you wake in the morning thinking "Please kids not yet."
And then change all the bedding cos the nappy's that wet.
When you drift down the stairs in a zombie like state,
Even though it's a reasonable quarter to 8.
As you turn on the kettle for that first caffeine fix,
Whilst sorting the juice, bottle, hoops, Weetabix.
When you finally sit down, they want bowl number two,
Don't worry about yours, it's not about you.
So now that the children are all fed and hydrated,
You deserve a minute, after all, you have waited.
So, you sit on your phone repeating the baby's name,
Hoping he'll listen, "Don't touch that picture frame!"
But he doesn't so back you are onto the floor,
Which is where you spend most of the day, you are sure.
And once you are down there, and you're starting to play,
You realise this is the best part of your day.
The giggles, the laughter, the joy in their face,
Who gives a shit toys are all over the place?
They can have all my energy, my food and my time,
Because I am their best friend,
And they're sure as hell mine.

***

Daddy said he'd appreciate a lie in this morning.
Daddy has been a father of 2 for 10 months now and still thinks I have control over this.
Daddy is stupid.

***

As I arose with the tribe this morning, I looked at Baby Tom's "bear hunt blanket friend" (as Bill calls it) and decided, today was the day. It needed to go in the wash...

I also felt like it provided an accurate metaphor for myself in its sad, dirty, food-stained state. Wet from dribble and covered in snot. Dragged around tirelessly day after day but anyway, I digress...

Safe to say, he's refused to nap without it and has drove me close to crazy throughout the day.

So, as it finally emerged from the dryer, looking and smelling fresh, I saw his little face light up as he began speed crawling towards being reunited with it. And I realised, it is a metaphor for me. It's there for him when he wakes in the morning. When he's tired or sad. When he's happily playing or out and about. It makes him feel safe.
And for a minute, I wanted to cuddle it.

Although, I quickly got over that when I remembered how I'm an adult now and I don't need a comforter.
And proceeded to bake a chocolate cake and open a bottle of wine.

***

Bill's day:
I'm awake, my tick tock hasn't got sunshine on it yet but I'm going to get up anyway because I do what I want, I'm almost 4, I'm an adult now.

I've explained to Mummy and Daddy that it's okay because my tick tock is asleep but I can just go downstairs and play on my tablet. Mummy muttered something under her breath and told me to do what I want so I went downstairs, played on my tablet and pissed all over the sofa.

It's a pretty normal day, I'll just demand juice and food constantly like usual. Mummy likes to make sure I'm fed and watered.

Just going to play with Baby Tom for a bit (mainly because he is heading towards my toys). I should play nice but I think I'll sit on his back, hit him in the head with a hammer and rugby tackle him to the floor whenever he tries to get up.

I want to play in my bedroom now, probably because Baby Tom is used to my shit and it doesn't make him cry anymore. And by play in my room, I mean, move some toys around, shit my pants, and then come back downstairs and hope no one notices.

Mummy can smell my poo poo pants. I think I'm about to get done...

Baby Tom's Day:
I'm awake, I want to play! I'll make some awake noises! Yay! Daddy is here! Oh, dummy is in, I'm drifting back to sleeeep...

Right, now I'm up! Let's cry!

Food... give me my bottle now! I'll just follow mummy around the kitchen screaming even though I can see she's making my bottle as fast as she can.

Now, breakfast please. I'd like breakfast now. I'll just follow mummy around the kitchen screaming even though I can see she's making it as fast as she can.

Now I'm tired. Been up a whole hour. Nap time.
When I wake up, I'll do the same for lunch, I'll probably just follow mummy around the kitchen screaming even though I can see she's making it as fast as she can.

Debbie's day:
Is that Baby Tom? It's okay, Daddy's going, thanks Daddy, it means a lot.
Is that Bill? Fucks sake tick tock hasn't said wake up time yet, but I can't be arsed, it's a problem for future me.
Baby Tom is up now, Christ I'm exhausted.

Coffee! Help me coffee!

My saviour, the positivity, the strength to survive the day quickly disappeared with the clumps of stale milk that glugged down the plug hole.
I mixed it with tears.

Feed everyone.
Tidy up.
Put a wash on.
Feed everyone again.
Dream about the days I'll not have piss and shit to clean up.
Feed everyone again - hang on, I've not eaten yet.

All I've wanted to do is nip to the shop, get some milk. It's <u>4pm</u>. I've still not been.

I can't wait to finally get some bloody milk, and then to pour myself a lovely, well-deserved glass of wine.

***

A poorly Baby Tom got us up around 4/5 times during the night. Lost count. I may have done a couple of dummy runs in my sleep, who knows?
At half 6 I decided it was time for some medicine. Calpol for him and perhaps a Diazepam for me?

I hurried back to his room praying his cries would not wake Bill to find Bill stood at the top of the stairs like the kid from The Omen and I shit myself a little bit.

He wanted to show me something. I shit myself a little bit more.

What could he possibly have to show me? A spider? A bird which had broken through the window? A monster hiding in his tent? All sorts going through my head. It was worse.
"I've been sick, look mummy."

Fantastic that. Have pasta at nursery did you? (Why is all kids food cooked in orange sauces?)
All over the bed, all over the drawers, all over the carpet, all over my sleep.

Honestly, I've felt like I'm pretty competent as a parent until right now when I realise I've not had much sick to deal with.

So, he's downstairs loving life and demanding breakfast, Baby Tom is going back to sleep, Daddy is up, and I'm wandering back and forth with some vanish not knowing exactly how to save the carpet but knowing I definitely need to.

Fair to say, with such a magnificent start to the day, I've been a complete arsehole to deal with since.

***

Today, I made some terrible choices.

1. I decided that whilst Bill was at nursery, I'd take Baby Tom to get his feet measured. Not a bad choice however I thought I'd go to Meadowhall to do this. In the school holidays. Rookie error.

2. I decided to wake Baby Tom from his nap, to set off immediately and to eat there as it was getting late and I didn't want to hit traffic on the way back. He cried all the way because he was hungry. And I hit traffic both ways.

3. I decided to go to McDonald's for dinner. In the school holidays. I thought that itself was the most horrific experience that I could possibly endure until I realised that I had to navigate a pushchair and a tray of food - complete with hot coffee - through what I can only explain as a menagerie of feral kids waiting impatiently for

their happy meals as their mothers hunted down seats for their young.

4. I decided, when someone stole the table I'd finally spied, that instead of remaining calm and laughing at the situation, I'd barge through the sea of prams and wheelchairs, hangrily knocking into chairs in a great struggle wheeling the pushchair with one hand and holding the tray in the other whilst loudly exclaiming "this is fucking ridiculous."

At this point, I actually made a wonderful decision.
I decided that tonight, I'm hitting the gin instead of the gym.
And peace was restored...

***

Motherhood is waking up exhausted and still getting shit done.

Motherhood is constantly feeding people, then realising <u>at 4pm</u> you've had nothing, scoffing on some chocolate whilst hiding in a corner and then having to suggest the kids have a delicious, tasty pear each when they ask for the treat you've just eaten.

Motherhood is telling a little person off for saying "Oh my God" instead of "Oh my goodness" despite muttering "for fucks sake" under your breath at an average rate of 8 times per hour throughout the day.

Motherhood is doing 4 loads of washing and then someone pissing their pants.

Motherhood is thinking, "Right, I've had a good go at parenting but I think it's run it's course now, no one can say I haven't tried but it's just not for me." Then ordering an Elf on a Shelf.

Motherhood is getting through the day, cracking open a bottle of wine, and reflecting on just how lucky you are to have the most amazing children in your life.

***

Had one of my all time favourite meals for lunch today. Cheese and spaghetti on toast. Beaut.

Asked Bill if he'd like in on the goods.
He said no. Quite angrily actually. Just wanted toast.

So... Preferences served. Baby Tom just got toast too. Whilst he can't talk, he gets what he's given and to be honest, I couldn't be arsed to sit at the table.

Like fucking flies round shit.

"Mmmmmm, Mummy, that looks so tasty!"

Both of them. Staring at me. Edging closer. Baby Tom opening his mouth in anticipation each time I filled my fork.
Audacity gained, Bill asks for some, after all "it's only sharing."

Only sharing! I'm basically eating liquid gold in this day and age.
Fuck off piglets.

Their faces filled with sorrow as I ate my own food.
I gave them some hoops.
I'm such a pushover.

I wasn't always like this.
I'm angry.
I need revenge.

So I sneaked into the toilet to eat a clandestine Creme Egg. Ha! Take that you gluttonous goblins.

***

There's not much that's quite as beautiful as looking over your child sleeping soundly before you go to bed.

And nothing quite as annoying as smelling shit as you do so...

***

"I was minding my own business. Causing no harm to anyone and blissfully unaware of the peril about to bestow upon me.

Then it happened.
Out of nowhere, I was taken.
Abducted in plain sight and forced into the depths of hell.

I was stripped naked and presented before another. He was less distressed. Almost comfortable. He must have been conditioned to deal with it. To accept what was about to happen.

I was terrified. Alone whilst in the presence of others. Vulnerable. Clinging on to the one who had taken me praying it wouldn't get any worse. Begging and pleading in cries and screams as my distress prevented the words from leaving my mouth.

I was offered an alternative.
Some sort of Chinese water torture.
I put up a fight.
A good one.
It made my abductor angry.

And then it happened.
I found myself back with the other.

The most traumatic experience of my entire life was about to intensify..."

Or at least that's how I imagine Baby Tom feels when I try to bath him.

***

Went for a quaint little walk with the kids.

quaint;
attractively unusual or old fashioned.
Similar to picturesque, charming, sweet.

disastrous;
causing great damage.
Similar to catastrophic, calamitous, ruinous.

That's more like it.
I went for a disastrous little walk with the kids.

***

A couple of things have happened today:

1. Bill woke up looking white as a ghost and then threw up. But don't worry, I called school to report his absence, gave him some paracetamol and he made a full recovery before he'd even swallowed it.
He's eaten everything he's seen since.

2. I got changed for the gym, remembered I'd not booked on, went to book, saw I'd missed the session and ordered a pizza instead.

Oh and 3. Baby Tom shit on my leg.

***

The young 'un's in nursery for a few hours settling in, I have a presentation to do, an approaching assignment deadline, half the house to deep clean and could do with cutting the grass.
Fuck it, I'm watching Netflix.

***

Today I feel like I've achieved nothing.
I woke up feeling unjustifiably exhausted and have been barely able to suppress a blazing, demonic, hormonal rage throughout the day. Today I wanted to change all the bedding; I haven't. I wanted to nip to the shop; I haven't. I wanted to shower; as yet, I still haven't.

Today, Bill has not left my side. I've literally tripped over him a number of times. Baby Tom has also disliked being too far from me crying when I've left the room.
Today I've kept them both safe, clean, fed and watered. And feeding them is full time job the little piglets... I've even fed myself a couple of times.

Today, as bedtime approaches and I'm desperately hoping Daddy wants to open a bottle of wine after tea, my children are having a whale of a time playing and laughing and giggling with each other. My house is tidy, the washing's away and all the daily chores are done.

Today, I've achieved a lot whilst feeling I've achieved nothing.

***

Is it frowned upon to leave the kids in the car for two minutes whilst I nip in the butchers if I park right outside the shop and have them within eyesight? Or to leave them at home unattended whilst

I stroll to the pub alone with my thoughts and drink two bottles of wine? Asking for a friend.

***

02:17 *hears crying* It's Bill.
Me: "What's the matter darling, are you okay?"
Bill: "I want to eat McDonald's"
Nice one. Thanks.

***

Procrastination at its finest is laying on the sofa watching 'Sofia the First' to find out if she manages to break the curse that's making her croak like a frog before she goes on stage to sing the national anthem at the festival. FYI Bill's in bed...

***

Anyone else feel a pang of guilt as they ship the kids off to Nan Nan and Grandad's for the night so they can go party?
Me neither... Freedom!!

***

Bill woke up crying last night. He couldn't tell me why. This morning he told me that a dinosaur T-Rex was getting at him and he had to run really fast like a cement mixer. But mummy couldn't help because I was outside and daddy was in bed so the dinosaur got him and he was inside it's tummy.
He's now watching Jurassic Park at his request.

***

People sometimes joke and ask which child is my favourite and I can honestly say, they both do my head in equally.

***

Once, when putting Bill to bed, I told him I was going for a jog later. He told me that I was too heavy to run.

***

Anyone ever wonder if the staff at your local shop recognise that you; dry shampooed (for the fourth day in a row), no makeup, fella's clothes on and kids in tow you and you; managed to attend to personal hygiene, face full of slap, dolled up for a night with no kids you are the same person?

And if you don't think they do, do you feel the need to tell them? Like, hey it's me! I'm not actually a stinking mess!?

***

Anyone else's kid get proper confused when they're watching actual TV and not something recorded?
Bill's like; I want that one on again. And can't comprehend that I'm not controlling it.
And there's always drama when adverts come on. "Mum! Your tele has come on again!" (*in his angry voice)
4 channels I had pal. I used to watch a bird with a chalkboard for an hour waiting for Sesame Street to start. Deal with it.

***

Bill: "I want my tablet please."

Me: "No, not until after breakfast."

Bill: "I don't want any breakfast, I had breakfast the other day"

Me: "Well you're not having your tablet until Mummy's phone makes a noise"
*sets alarm for 10:00

Me: "Want some breakfast Bill?"

Bill: "Yes please Mummy."

***

In Tesco, pick a steak up, Bill starts wailing uncontrollably.

What could possibly be the matter?

He didn't want Daddy to have anything for tea obviously.

Sound.

***

I've actually had a lovely day today.

Well, I've been finishing the deep cleaning I started yesterday but I managed to time everything perfectly so that I did so mainly interruption free which is lovely.

So, I wonder; how can one day be so idealistic and yet others be so unnecessarily stressful?

Maybe the young one's teeth aren't as troublesome for him today?

Perhaps it's me? Maybe my hormones are particularly well balanced today?

Or… And then it hits me!
Bill's been at nursery. I've only had one kid to deal with.

Dear single child families; don't do it!
Unless of course you enjoy frequent anxiety sweats, a feeling of tiredness so severe you're praying it's due to low iron levels because this can't be normal, and shouting. A lot.

***

1 year ago today, Bill was released from his night cage and transitioned into a big boy's bed.

I remember that first night. Praying he wouldn't get up in the night and start scavenging around... He didn't.

To this day, he has never let himself out of his bedroom. When he awakes, he gets up and plays with his toys or I often find him standing at his bed reading a book. If he would like to leave, he knocks on the door from the inside and waits for me to set him free.

It's one of the many things I love about him.

***

It's often said that when Mummy is stressed, the children can sense it and become stressed too. And that it's not good for anyone involved.

I'd like to argue that when Mummy is not stressed, the children can sense it, and think "Watch this!" because they fucking thrive off it. The absolute demons.

***

I've never been one of these 'let's go out and do something' types. I much prefer to fester on the sofa most days whatever the weather.

Daddy thinks I should be outside more with the kids. Particularly the bigger one. I mean, he's probably got a point but I'm getting right into Paw Patrol recently and well, blah...

So, the other day I had a wonderful idea.
I could stand Bill outside and get him to start running. When he did, I could trip him over.

Daddy would get home, see his poorly knee, and ask what happened.
Bill would relay the story of how he was running outside and he fell over.
He'd not be lying, Daddy would think we've been playing outside, I wouldn't have to get dressed or otherwise exert myself. Winners all round?

***

Daddy's gone out on the razzle with the lads and God knows if he'll ever make it back.

We dropped him at the train station. Cue Bill sobbing his little heart out watching Daddy merrily skip off into the distance because he "wants to go on the Choo Choo with Daddy and his daddy friends".

On the way home, as we neared the glistening light of those inviting Golden Arches, Bill's frown was turned upside down as he exclaimed; "You see that Mummy? What's Old Donald's doing? Let's go and look!"

Safe to say that now we're back at home, Bill's only worry is that he wants to eat his sausage before his pancakes but it's a "bit hot".

Doesn't give a shit about Daddy anymore.

***

It's not often that me and the kids sit out in the garden in the sunshine. And every time we do, I remember why.

Firstly, there's the sunscreen application. I hate sunscreen. I also hate cleaning the kitchen floor. So I was particularly displeased when whilst conducting one of Bill's 80 toilet trips a day, Baby Tom, who's still army crawling, came to find us like a great, giant snail leaving behind him a trail of sticky factor 50.

Then, there's the garden itself. Like a hostile jungle with its foot high nettles. So, I have to cut that before we're out in it. Another of my favourite tasks. Not. And now there's grass everywhere. Literally. Except in the lawnmower compartment it's meant to be in. I did front and back lawns and there was nothing in it when I'd finished.

Bill wants to play in the water. Okay. Paddling pool is out. Only I don't have a pump. So I spend a solid 20 minutes blowing it up manually. Almost blackout twice. Probably did once.

It's now almost <u>2 o'clock</u>. 4 hours since I first applied the sun cream. So obviously they need some more on. Oh and dinner. I have to feed them too... Ffs.

Half two. We're out! Grass is cut, cream is on, swimming attire sorted, sun hats on heads, pool inflated and filled with water (and grass), water pistols at the ready... let the fun begin!!

It's not fun. Bill's rugby tackling Baby Tom and almost drowning him, then, when I tell him off for it, Baby Tom is trying to drown himself. Everyone is covered in grass and bugs. Now Bill needs his 56th piss of the day. And if you think I'm about to drag two dripping wet, grass covered kids through the house to get one to the toilet you're very wrong. You're peeing in the garden mate. Get in the corner.

Finally, I sit down. The boys are having a lovely time together, the sun is still shining. This. This is why I've don't it all... Oh wait. That lasted 5 minutes. Baby Tom is tired now. I get him dried off, nappy on, laid in the pram in the shade. Bill's took himself to the corner again for wee 57. And now, he wants to go back inside because it's a bit too sunshiny and a bit hot.

It took 4.5 hours to experience 5 minutes of enjoyment and now, I have a paddling pool to empty, clean and let down, two kids to bath, the entire house to hoover and the kitchen floor to steam.

And I'm exhausted.
And I still don't have a tan.
And they need feeding again very soon.

God I wish this was wine...

***

Bill, who usually gets up around half 7/8ish, was knocking on his door at 05:50 this morning. I shouted permission for egress and he excitedly bound into my room ready for the day. This excitement was rapidly diffused upon meeting myself, half asleep in bed, like the sloth that I am as I greeting my little cherub with a simple (yet firm) "No!"

He immediately began sobbing his little heart out as "it's wake up time Mummy" and so being the kind, loving, selfless mother that I am, I gave him his tablet and had another hours kip.

***

Anyone have some earplugs? Or a shotgun? Or a black fucking hole that these noisy bastard kids can run into?

***

I believe that in order to ensure your children grow up to be decent human beings, consistency (amongst other things) is key.
Empty threats teach only that rules can be broken so if you can't follow through on something, don't say it.

Today, Bill emptied the toys out all over the room saying that he wanted to make a mess. I told him this was fine providing he tidied up afterwards which he agreed to. At least until that time came.

He was so proud of himself. Singing "I've made a m-ess, na-na na na-na-na!"

When he sat down, away from the plastic carnage he'd created, I asked him to put everything away. I asked very politely a number of times. Each response of "No" getting angrier until it progressed into kicking and throwing things. Fuck this!

Here comes the threat; "Put all these toys away now or they're going in the bin!"

Usually this is enough. Today, it was not.

Apparently, he wasn't bothered. "Put them in the bin" he says... Well son, I don't think you quite know who you're dealing with.

I grab a bin bag, he's still not bothered.
I pick up a toy, he still doesn't care.

Right, that's one in. I start picking up all the broken ones and happy meal toys (might as well have a clear out) and he starts crying. Good! It's working. But it's still not enough. He still won't come and tidy up. So he gives me no choice, one of his favourite Owlette figurines is next within my reach.
He looks at me, I look at him, we both look at Owlette.

I can't back down now.
He can't see me as weak.
I'm doing it for the greater good.

She's gone, they're all in the bin, he's sobbing his heart out, but he's come to tidy up.

It's all about boundaries mate.
And I'll always win.

***

Today, we dropped the big one off at nursery and then took the little one to Grandma's. As she lifted the car seat out and closed the car door, we wheel spun back into 2014 where going out for lunch and day drinking was a thing and it's been bloody lovely. Here's to nostalgia, it's not what it used to be.

***

We've made it almost 4 years without any real behavioural difficulties from Bill but sadly, it appears that our lucky streak has ended.

This last couple of weeks have brought frequent bouts of rage in the form of aggressive behaviours and to be completely honest, my usual methods of addressing such incidents are ceasing to have any impact.

Today however, fate stepped in...

15 minutes after I put Bill on the stairs, where he continued to stamp his feet and hit the wall, lunging at me with the devil in his eyes if I approached him, a visitor came to the door.

The perfect time to play my first "Right, this man has come to take you to where the naughty boys go" card.

And Bill absolutely shit himself.

Hopefully for long enough to pass this difficult stage. I want my pleasant little boy back.

***

Bill: "I'm hungry"
Me: "Okay, would you like a cheese sandwich?"
Bill: "Yes please."
Me: "Do you want hard cheese or cheese slices?"
Bill: "Chocolate."

***

Bill's just burst into singing a bit of Frank Sinatra.

It's crackers what they pick up on. You can literally teach them anything.

I'm currently telling him that his middle name is Horatio. Just for a laugh.

***

Today has been a hard day.

One of the most challenging since becoming a parent. Absolute meltdown galore and the worst behaviour I've ever witnessed from my almost 4 year old. I've come so close to completely losing my shit on numerous occasions and it really made me question my abilities as a mother.

I've had to consciously remind myself that it's just a phase and that it shows normal, healthy emotional development but Christ it's been a struggle.

As I reflect now, I think about how my boys are both happy, warm, fed, watered and safely tucked up in their beds. And how despite shouting at Bill more than once (and probably louder than I should have) he still told me how much he loves me before I left him to go to sleep.

I've also remembered how he's called me Batman all day. And that even when I don't feel like I'm winning at parenting, I'm still a superhero in his eyes.

So in case anyone else needs to hear this today; the fact that you care means you're doing amazing.

(*must buy bigger wine glasses…)

***

Baby Tom often stirs just after 6 but if you make a quick dummy run, you can usually squeeze another hour out of him.

This started to wake Bill who would then immediately bang on his bedroom door for permission to leave and get up for the day.

Well, I'm lazy. And I want that extra hour. So we bought a 'special clock'.

It's been working great! The sunshine comes up <u>at 07:45</u> and Bill's straight out of bed, knocking on his door then bolting through into our room <u>at 07:46</u> excitedly exclaiming "It's wake up time because the sunshine is up!"

The only issue was that one nursery morning, when we have to get up earlier the sunshine hadn't come up yet which caused a major meltdown (welcome to our world kid...)
Anyway, Daddy's shitty stealth skills meant that Bill witnessed him manually wake up the sunshine.

So after many, long and thorough conversations about how for nursery, like for mummy and daddy when going to work, we sometimes have to get up before the sunshine because that means we're big boys and girls, Bill has learnt that he can just get up when he wants and wake the sunshine up himself.

"Mummy, the sunshine hasn't come up itself but it's okay because I did it now."

***

Some days you really think you're smashing it at parenting. Then one shits in the freshly changed nappy and the other walks mashed potato into the carpet all as Iggle Fucking Piggle is singing his name for the 100,000th time today and you find yourself back in full on psycho mode.

***

"Where's that gorgeous boy?" I say to Baby Tom as I hold him up to see his reflection in the mirror.

"I'm in here Mummy!" Shouts Bill from the other room.

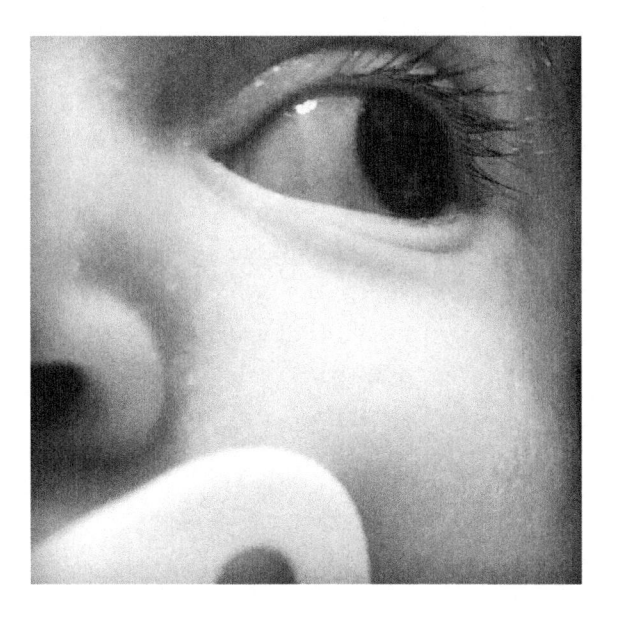

***

Experienced my first kids party today.
Of course, I've been to kids parties before, but this was the first of the 'invitation from a stranger type'.

Remembered to buy a card and a present which surprised me.
Rocked up with a hangover which didn't.

It was going well, tea and coffee service for the parents, we were even invited to sample the buffet.

Spent time sat at the back of the hall, awkwardly exchanging pleasantries with other lone parents so as not to be rude. Each of us hating it as much as the other, we all returned to our phones after the whole, "Which one's yours then?" because there really is nothing else to say.

Still, it was going well.

How naive I was.

No one told me that the hell of a kids party comes as it's over. Trying to explain to a sugar filled whirlwind that it has to get off the bouncy castle and return home to a land free of balloons and soft play paraphernalia is a nightmare.

Then, just to rub salt in the wound, after literally dragging the screaming beast off the inflatable nemesis, consoling him only with the thought of eating some yummy cake when he gets home if he gets his shoes on nicely and stops crying, you find a whistle in the party bag.

A fucking whistle.

What sort of prick does this to fellow parents?
You just wait until I'm inviting yours to our parties Hun.
Where can I bulk buy recorders?

***

Bought annual passes to the Yorkshire Wildlife Park today. Lovely place and relatively close by so was an easy decision to make.

Couple of things annoy me though.

Firstly, the parents that try to push past me to allow their 9 month old to see the animals better.

They don't care mate, not one bit. In fact Bill's been enough times now that seeing a real life lion was much less interesting than the bubbles in the water. At one point, as we were all "Look over there Bill, it's a rhino!" He was like, "Look Mummy and Daddy, some tables on the other side!"

The point is, the kids don't give a shit really. And it's me that just forked out £170 on passes.

Also, after our lovely, exciting family day out, I asked Bill what his favourite bit was.
He replied, "The cookie."

***

Current situation:

Picking the cheese off the cheese on toast Bill demanded because he doesn't want cheese on it.

Cheese on toast with no cheese is just toast you dumb fuck.

***

Special shout out to the grandparents who fed Bill 8 biscuits for tea.

Put him to bed at 7 and so far, he's found his long lost seahorse and picked a wart off.

Nice one.

***

Toddlers; forever saying cute things you love to hear.
Like, "Mummy, I just put my hands down the toilet."

***

Survived another kids party today!

Surprising really as initially we turned up at the wrong venue. Luckily there wasn't a party there - that could have been awkward, I don't think I'd have noticed.

Lovely to see my child all excited, running into a room full of other people's children (eurgh...) and recognising his pals.
Also lovely to see the birthday boy shyly hide away from everyone whilst clinging desperately onto his mother's legs for hours. It's always nice to know it's not just yours that displays such annoying behaviour.

Wasn't so happy about the fact that Bill refused to participate in any of the activities without me.
I'll openly admit that my plan was to turn up, ignore people as much as possible whilst watching my darling play from afar and checking on my phone.
Performing the Agadoo, Hokey Cokey and Conga in front of a load of strangers weren't on my list of things to do today.

Also found out that there was a second party today that we weren't invited to. Thanks Lily, we didn't want to come anyway... Also, you're off the Christmas card list.

End scene; the 'magician', whose only magic trick was to transport the parents back to the parties they attended as children, handed out sword shaped balloons. Obviously, due to my earlier, however reluctant participation in the 'fun', the little people perceived me as one of their own and charged at me.
Fantastic.

Tonight, the wine is gin.

***

Being a mum is going out for lunch and finding a pair of your kids shit stained pants in your pocket from 4 days ago.

***

When do you stop checking on your kids at night?

Is it when they tell you to fuck off?
Or when their wives do?

***

One day a mother of two young boys found that she wanted them to spend the day in their garden together.
The sun was shining down gloriously. So gloriously in fact that it appeared to be worth the preparation such an idea entailed.

Now in order for this mother to actually enjoy the day in their garden together, entertainment had to be provided. Mainly because wanting to 'spend the day in the garden together' actually meant trying her damnedest to spend at least an hour reading a book and catching some rays whilst the boys entertained themselves and/or each other.

This meant it necessary for the paddling pool. Now you may remember from the last day in the garden, that this was an absolute farce. She had to manually blow up the pool, almost passed out a few time's, got bit to death by a plague of midges and 5 minutes after it was ready, the ungrateful offspring wanted to go inside. But! We as humans try to learn from our mistakes so this time, she was much better prepared and sat down to manually blow the chuff up so she didn't feel as light headed.
*must buy a bloody pump.

Anyway this time was much better! The children both got so excited, they loved helping her fill it with water and they played beautifully together. It was so wonderful to watch that she didn't even want to read her book. What a lovely day in the garden. Living their best lives. Having a right laugh. Until...

Baby Tom gets out whinging. No biggie. He can go down for a nap. He's absolutely knackered actually.

Then she sees it. A wet, brown smudge where the swimming nappy meet his leg. Thank God she put that on. Except it's not done much really. The water in the paddling pool is tinged with shit and smells like sewage and inside the nappy, which obviously doesn't hold water and is leaking onto everything it touches, including her leg, is some sort of horrific beef stew and dumplings. Only the dumplings are made of human faeces. And there's no beef. Or stew.

Now her zen like state is swiftly switched to psycho. Especially as Bill is about to jump back into the poo pool. I'm sure her neighbours thoroughly enjoyed experiencing such a drastic change in ambiance and have subsequently diagnosed her with Bipolar Disorder.

Regardless. She sorts it. Like a boss. Albeit a crazed one. And the little boy is down. The big one happy to be playing alone. Time is finally hers.

That is until the bin men come.

It's recycling day and Baby Tom is terrified of the sound of glass bottles being emptied into the truck. Half a second after her happy, ready to relax sigh, Baby Tom is screaming. The most terrified scream. It's actually quite ridiculous.
So off she goes to soothe him. Staring into the garden through the window at the book she started 8 months ago and still hasn't barely touched.

And of course just as he begins to settle, they empty hers. Which is obviously the fullest, and therefore loudest on the street. Best start filling it up for next time...

***

I stand at the sink washing the pots and reflect on my day.

It's been lovely. We've played, we've giggled, we've snuggled, the little people have even eaten everything I've provided for them.
It's 17:30 and I've not screamed at anyone yet.
A new PB.

The blissful feeling of pride and achievement warms my maternal soul like the dishwater warms my hands.

And it's actually quiet. Big lad is on his tablet and the little one is relaxing on the sofa, just about ready for bed, dummy in mouth and Bear Hunt Blanket friend in hand.

At least that's what I thought...

The smallest, who I'm sure is actually some sort of feral animal, has snook into the dining area like a silent, slithering snake and has stolen the forbidden tree off the side table.
He's slithered back and proceeded to create a mud bath party with his new found fern friend.
Merrily dancing around in the dirt as the sprigs of despair lay dying, along with my sense of accomplishment, in the cream carpet.

He then has the audacity to act surprised as I enter and exclaim in horror.
Big one still blissfully unaware of life, lost in the fictional world of Sonic the Hedgehog.

Fuck my life.

***

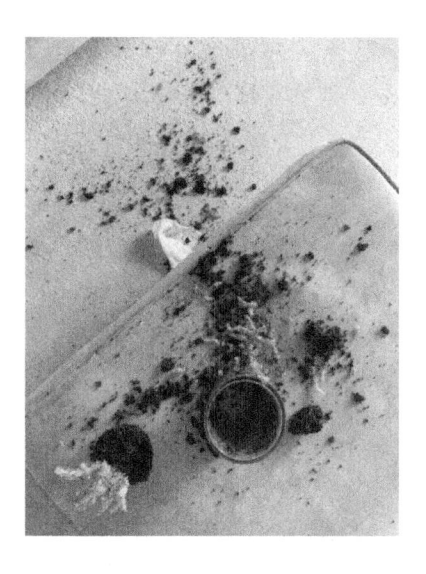

Wednesday's are big chore days and always super busy.

I'm knee deep into it, I've tidied the entire house, cleaned the kitchen, started sorting the mountain of washing and just about to tackle the bathroom.

Kids fed and watered. Big one all about to Netflix and chill with his blanket (because despite being 20 degrees he's "a little bit cold" apparently) and little one ready for a nap. Everything is on schedule.

Until the phone rings.
It's Daddy.
"There's been a terrible misunderstanding..."

I need to be at nursery for big lad's leaving party half an hour ago. No one is dressed. He starts balling like a baby because he doesn't want to go.

Rushing like I've never rushed before - because I've paid a tenner for this - within 5 mins the kids are dressed and happy and in the car and in no time at all big lad is at his party.
The Hawaiian theme has gone out of the window mind. But I'm sure we can have a lovely outfit ready for him by next week when we thought the party was...

I don't deal with nursery much as they go when I'm at work. But whenever I do go, I'm rushed, stressed, unorganised and look like a hobo.
Not even brushed my teeth or had a wash today.
That's a new low.

Anyway, I'd just like to make a few points clear:
1. I can be an organised mother.
2. I do usually attend to my personal hygiene.
3. It's almost always Daddy's fault.

***

Today, as I nipped upstairs to run the kids' bath, I could hear the most beautiful sounds of joy and laughter downstairs as they played with Daddy.

Such wonderment ended abruptly when it was followed by an exclamation of "Mummy, there's shit on the sofa!"

***

So that's the big lad all set and ready for his first day at school tomorrow.

Parents often feel so emotional about their children starting school.
I feel different to most.
I'm not one of these 'oh stop growing' types.
It's par for the course.

I'm excited for him. I can't wait to hear all about his day. For him to make new friends. For all the new knowledge and skills he'll learn.

I'm confident in our parenting so far and the wonderful little man he's already become.
That he will be well behaved yet still have fun, that he'll be kind to others, that he'll not stand for any shit when he knows he's right in doing so.

I'm sure we'll be telling you many times, but these are the best years of your life.

***

Week two of school done!
Bill still loves it.
But being a school mum... yeah, it's not for me.

***

Week three of the school run.
Baby Tom was in the pram ringing one of those "Ring for Prosecco" bells the entire way.

#mumgoals

***

Bill was crying when I picked him up from school today because he didn't have any homework.
Fucking geek.

***

I officially like the school run more than half term.

And I hate the school run.

***

I didn't want to spend the day dealing with laundry today.

So last night after work, I took a proactive approach and did two loads, meaning after a quick blast in the dryer this morning I'd be free from it.

So obviously, to help out, both kids pissed the bed.

***

I wake up most mornings exhausted. Like a mardy teenager begging for 10 more minutes.
Something the offspring don't appear to comprehend.

I make a coffee and expect to be able to drink it in peace whilst I come around and wake up for the day. The kids fail to respect this also.

Some people get dressed, some don't.
Some have a wash and brush their teeth, some won't.
Often there's yelling and tears.
Often from me.

I have an incessant need to maintain order and cleanliness. An unrealistic expectation with two small children and their hurricane of a father.

I'm completely neurotic.
Unreasonably at times.

My daily coffee intake has at least doubled.
I probably drink too much wine.

I don't always eat properly.

I'm one of those 'permanently exhausted pigeon' types, although I'm more like some sort of haggard troll.

Something has to change...

So obviously, I no longer drink cows milk.
I can't actually be a psycho.
It has to be some other cows hormones.

***

Young 'un calls his hot water bottle his "warm friend" and I feel that this is something we all need to keep in our lives.

***

My babiest boy.

He loves flowers.
He loves to sniff them - although he actually blows on them... it's cute.

His older brother also loves flowers.
He told me once how he was at the shop with Daddy and suggested they get me some, which I'd have loved.
However, I never received any...

Apparently, Daddy said it's okay, I just get my own.

***

How I feel:
Each morning I wake up exhausted.
The kids drive me crazy.
Someone always wants feeding.
I always have laundry to do.
Something always needs cleaning or tidying.
No one ever makes the beds.
Someone's always laid on me.
Someone's always shouting 'Mum'.
Their dad is just as hard to look after at times.
I shout too much.

What it means:

Each morning I wake up.
I have two happy and healthy children.
We have adequate food.
We have plenty of clothes.
We have our own house.
We have a safe space to sleep in.
My children want to be close to me.
My children miss me when I'm not there.
I have a wonderful partner.
I'm passionate?

***

I was tired, mardy and stressed this morning.
Then my son brought me some masterpiece made of car tracks.
"Mummy, I've made you a necklace and a crown because you're the Queen."

I wore them with pride.

***

Baby Tom has had one of those days.

One of those random outburst of unnecessary screaming days.
One of those "No" days.
One of those "I'm going to demand a treat every 30 seconds and kick of royally when I don't get one" days.
One of those I'm knackered so just as I'm drifting into a sweet slumber, I'll jump up and 'act goat' again for another hour days.

I'm having one of those <u>16:30</u> gin days.

***

Bill picked me a flower at play time.
His pockets doesn't keep much alive.
Still, it's better than the worm he brought me.

***

Bill got a Proud Peacock sticker today.

He stormed out of school like a moody teenager with a face like thunder.
Usual Thursday behaviour.

My back was about to break from carrying a 4 stone screaming Baby Tom who refused to walk as he'd refused to nap until 10 mins before we had to set off.
Usual Thursday behaviour.

Bill's teacher nipped out and asked if I had a minute.
She ran back in and came back with this.

Bill has wrote a story unaided.
From his own imagination.
With his own spelling.

She told me how super proud of him she is and explained that his handwriting is top end of year expectations.

I'm also super proud of him.
So, I'm having a celebratory gin once he's in bed.
Which to be fair, is usual Thursday behaviour.

10 points if you can work out what it says...

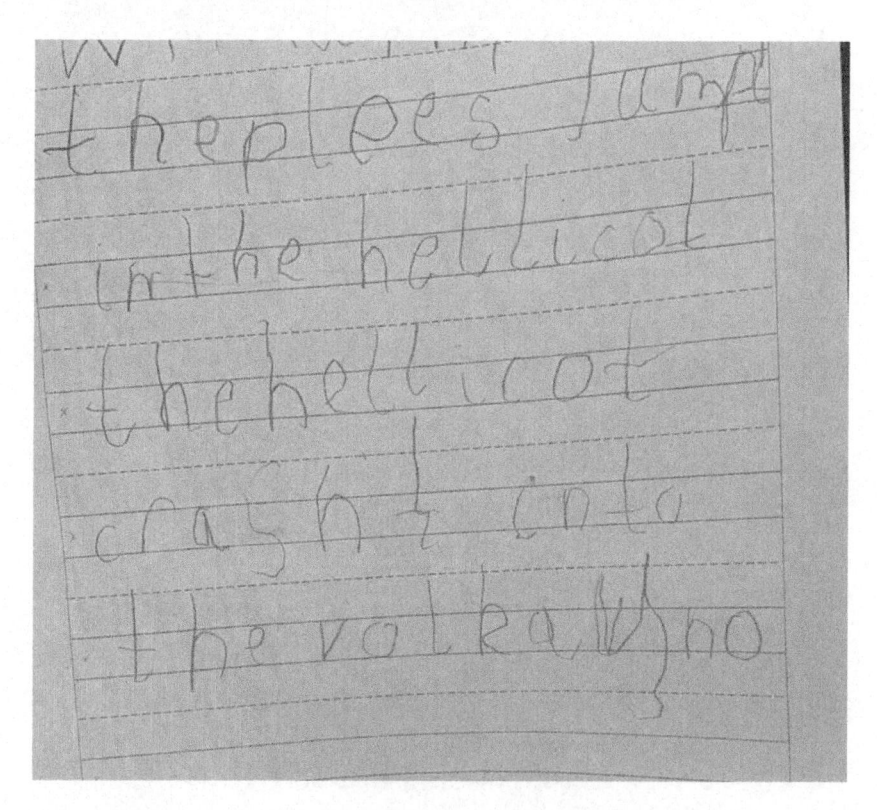

***

Last night I went out with the girls.
Naturally, because of the unnatural talent I have for drinking my own body weight in wine, I'm feeling somewhat hungover today.

FOOD is all I can think about.
I want to binge disgustingly on all the dirty foods I can get hold of.

The Colonel sorted us out for lunch with his finger licking goodness straight from the chicken Gods but I want more. I need more.

So I'm sat with the lads thinking how I need to feed them too. The thought of getting off my fat arse and banging some nuggets in the oven is all a bit much. CBA. Surely it's not okay to feed the kids multiple takeaways in one day…

"Who wants Old Donald's for tea?"
There.
I said it out loud.
No going back now.
Piss off Karen.

Only my local Golden Arches aren't online right now and I can't place an order. Ffs.

Maybe this is a sign.
My young children weren't meant to have a McDonalds a couple of hours after a KFC.

So I pulled myself together, emptied my mind of all McThoughts and did the right thing.

I ordered a Fridays instead.

***

It's not unknown on a <u>Saturday afternoon</u> for us to find a nice spot to visit for a family walk. Today was no exception.

We'd heard of a lovely nature reserve about 30 minutes drive away, so off we went.

Found it.
Got parked.
Baby Tom had a nap on the way.
Winning.

Beautiful place. Lovely weather. Stunning views. I quickly realised there probably wouldn't be anywhere to grab a coffee but I could deal with that.

Kids found a big hill to roll down, and just like them, it all spiralled out of control from there...

We entered the woods, lots of trees to climb, hundreds of sticks to pick up, the blissful babble of the brook beside us. Beautiful. But then the branches of the trees became more invasive, the path narrowed, the ground became steeper and increasingly uneven. Not the best place to be with a child and a toddler. Especially when they're refusing to walk.

We decided to head back.
Long story short, we didn't make it back.
We ended up in a field, lost, hot, tired and hungry. Be a good place for a coffee hut actually...
Retraced our steps again.
Back to the supposed safety of the unsteady woodland trail.
Cliff like faces mocking us from the left and tree roots begging us to plunge into the stream to the right.

And then finally, we found some steps.

Shining golden in the sunlight as if they led straight up to the pearly gates.
We were saved!

Or were we?
Well no, the answer is we were not.
It was even more unsafe.
Led along the side of the A1.
We walked for what seemed like miles.
I'm sure I could see the Angel of the North at one point.

It's not until this point we remember it's 2021 and we have access to a map and GPS.
We're over an hours walk away from the car.
The kids are knackered and getting hungry.
There's no pavement and cars are speeding past.
Only one thing to do.

Our Lass ran for the car.
Leaving myself and his children, everything he holds dear in the world, at the side of the road like abandoned dogs until he could return valiantly, riding his metal stead.
Rescuing his entire family and somehow saving the day after he got us lost in the first place.

Still not had a coffee.
Opting for something a little stronger.

***

Do you get what I mean about how shit Thursday's are? Kids are knackered and go next level psycho on a Thursday.

I woke up feeling motivated. Feeling ready. Feeling badass.

Got loads done this morning.

Was waiting for a shower when the young un fell asleep, he was nodding <u>around 10am</u>.
Winner!

Or not...

<u>13:30</u>. Still no nap. Still no shower.
The thought of the school run, looking and smelling like a hobo loomed over me like a lemon drizzle cake does someone on a diet.

Then I heard a bang.
The tumble dryer blew up.
Fantastic!

This wine saved me from a fridge/freezer full of waste actually. And I've just done a big shop.
I saw some wine on the side and thought fuck it, I'm having that tonight I'll bang it in the fridge. Which was turned off.
Dryer has tripped the electrics but not turned the TV off so I didn't realise.
*wine saves lives...

Managed a shower.
Locked the door so Baby Tom couldn't escape to go live his best life.

Did school run with wet hair, hence the state of it now.
He ran the whole way like a turbo charged bipolar on a manic episode. Cute really, didn't mind that.

Bill hated the fact that we had to go home.
Because obviously he'd rather be homeless and sleep in a park he thinks is round the corner, even though it's not, but who the hell am I to tell him it's actually a car drive away and he's confused.

Got home, they all screamed over who got to sit on the left side of the stairs to take their shoes off. Then argued for a good 3 minutes each time an advert came on because "I wish that I had that" means the other can't (none are having any of it).

Three poos and 7 trips to return them to bed later I'm settled with said life saving wine.

Stay tuned for next weeks episode.

***

Bill. This kid.
This beautiful, funny, intelligent, kind and caring boy.

He's just been shouting "Mummy" at the top of his voice.
I swiftly sprung to action and ran upstairs to aide my first born with whatever trauma faced him.
(Okay I said ffs, had another swig of beer and stomped upstairs…)

Upon opening the door, I found him sat upright in bed with a massive grin on his face asking "Do I look funny mummy?"
With 9 pairs of pants on his head.

***

Another typical Thursday:

05:45 I awake and immediately jump to silence my alarm so not to wake anyone else. Regretting the decision to arise early for a gym session in the constant battle against my ever slowing metabolism, I chose to fight the urge to drift back into slumber and get my ass 'up and at 'em'.

06:20 I stand at the squat rack yawning gapingly, caring not one ounce that Mr Motivator, who's obviously on some speed based pre-workout, has the audacity to stand blatantly judging my half-heartedness despite his full room takeover for a body weight circuit workout he could do at home.

07:40 I return home to a raging Baby Tom who appears to have been possessed by Lucifer himself during the night. He's also pissed the bed. Obviously intentionally as he saw how pleased I was that I'd washed, dried, ironed and put away every item of washing yesterday.

08:20 Daddy agrees that Bill can go to school on his scooter. An uninteresting aside you may think. However people, this is where it all went wrong as you'll soon see if you've not seen already…

13:15 Baby Tom, who I've spent the morning settling and distracting in an attempt to decrease the anger roaring through his veins, falls asleep on the sofa.

14:00 I treat myself to an uninterrupted shower. As I step out, I even decide to wear actual clothes for when I venture on the school run. As I stand staring into the abyss of my wardrobe, I remember that my legs resemble those of a yeti so opt for jeans. Another terrible decision that I've not even realised yet.

14:45 I 'accidentally' wake Baby Tom in preparation for the school run. He screams "No Mummy!" at the top of his surprisingly large lungs and I stare at him in awe of the beauty I've created… Okay, I wandered into the kitchen muttering "Here we fucking go" but hey, that's how I'm choosing to remember it.

14:55 The elephant style memory of two year olds means that Baby Tom is much more obliging than usual to leave to house to get his brother as he'd like to go on his scooter. I too am much more obliging and allow him as I envision the return journey, Bill on his, the arguments, the stress. It wasn't worth it.

14:56 We've still not left the driveway.

14:57 We're still in the road immediately at the end of the driveway.

15:03 We've made it as far as the next door neighbours.

15:05 The man washing his car a few houses up has a good old chuckle. The lady running past (who's ran 3 laps of the field at this point) passes me an empathetic glance.

15:10 No amount of coercion, bribery or down right humiliating begging will do anymore. I'm actually going to be late picking up my son from school. I pick him up. Surfboard style. Carrying him under one arm and the scooter under the other. He's kicking and screaming. I want to be. And of course it's at the precise moment I'm loaded up like Buckaroo that the clouds mysteriously disappear revealing the blazing sun, shining down gloriously onto me, in my jeans, sweating like a mother fucker and carrying my child like I've kidnapped him as I ran to make it to school in time.

15:15 Baby Tom continues. People in the school yard don't even pretend not to see me anymore. They stand staring at me, a mother broken. Sweating in places my gym session didn't even moisten. Only now, I have two children and two scooters to contend with.

15:20 Baby Tom still refuses to walk or be carried, opting for his scooter. He scoots along at a speed that defies all the scientists have ever taught us because I'm sure time goes in reverse when he's on it.
Bill however has got good on his. He's off. Which is truly fantastic as I weave in and out of a menagerie of school mums and other people's children.

15:21 I'm still sweating, I'm wearing a mask, I feel like I'm not getting enough oxygen and I'm pretty sure I was getting flash backs of being told off for screaming too loud in the concrete tunnel at nursery when I was 4. Another empathetic glance catches my eye as I'm overheard pleading with the children to "Please let's just get out of the playground and into an open space".

15:25 We eventually make it up stream. I probably smell a bit like a salmon at this point. Bill mentioned the park and an ice cream.
Three things enter my mind:
1. If I get them an ice cream, I can pick up a bottle of wine.
2. If we go to the park, it will tire them out for bed and I can get them down nice and early.
3. It's a negotiation tool.
So despite my better judgement, we walk even further from home in the direction of the shop.
Baby Tom still being an utter arsehole, but Bill I must say is being a superstar, so unfair to deprive him of an ice cream and some park time. Again, this good behaviour probably a manipulative effort to guilt me into making this whole experience even shitter.

15:30 We make it to the shop. I decide there's no way in hell I'm carrying two scooters around in there, not with both kids and the unreasonably slim aisles. I set them on the floor outside. Bill starts crying. They may get stolen. I'd love that to be honest.
We enter, pick ice creams (and wine), of course there's a queue. And Baby Tom wants his ice cream immediately. His screams filling the ears of all those around me. And I'm stood there not giving a fuck carrying nothing but a bottle of wine. Mum goals!

15:35 We have a minute outside the shop. The boys open their ice creams, Bill's breaks, he cries, blah blah. Piss off man, I'm hiding my wine in your school bag...
I balance the two scooters on me like I've some strange Jenga challenge going on and off we trot to the park. But, can we go to the one on the way home? The one outside our house? Of course not. Ffs. They want to go to the other one. I want a bloody Diazepam at this point.

But in the name of motherhood, and keeping the peace, and just needing a break from the turmoil, off we go again in the wrong direction.

15:45 To be fair, the park bit was okay. They played nicely, until it was time to leave of course. At that point it took all my my strength and will, maternal instincts, moral compass (and the fact that two people had waltzed up dressed in black trousers and T-shirts with work badges on looking all 'Social Services' like), not to sit on the bench and drink the wine out of my 5 year olds school bag like a year 7 desperately needing a crisp sip of Lilt in a science lesson.

16:15 We're on our way home. The journey home was much like the journey to school, lots of tears, kicking, screaming, surf boarding and bizarre scooter balancing acts. But 4 hours later we finally made it.

16:40 Kids wanted pizza. The only thing we didn't have. Children meet Dominos, Dominos, these are the children. Fuck off Karen.

18:00 We're finally getting settled. Everyone's fed and dressed and ready for bed. Only as we snuggled together on the sofa, a trick I've found handy for getting Baby Tom down when he's overtired, the only person to fall asleep is me.
Nice one.

19:15 Eight trips upstairs later I'm drinking a wine I don't even want to be honest. I want to go to bed. There's a charity van coming round tomorrow though, reckon I can give them to them?

***

The Wednesdayest Thursday ever.

Don't get me wrong, there's been frequent defiance, nap refusals, clothing change related meltdowns and arguments over treats.

But nothing leading to the questioning of my life choices or if motherhood is really for me.

The boys have even played nicely.
Bill was teaching Baby Tom how to draw.
It was heart-warming.

I mean, I could go on to talk about how although 'football' is coming home, Our Lass made no attempt to do so last night but let's leave it on a positive eh?

***

Do you know what, the kids have been amazing. They've played lovey all day, we've been for a little bike ride for ice creams and then had the water squirters out in the garden and a picnic tea. But you lot don't like to see me winning at life on a Thursday. You sadists. So let's talk about the garden shall we…

I'm sure you've heard the saying, if you want anything doing, do it yourself.
Personally, where possible, if I want anything doing, I pay someone else to do it.

So I hired a gardener.
He did a wonderful job.
Unfortunately however, for a number of reasons, he's not been able to make it recently.

But I have a gardener.
So am I chuff cutting it myself.

Anyway, three weeks pass and opening the patio doors was like venturing into an unknown world. Jungle is massive.
The children wanted to play outside.
I'd have lost them in the towering weeds.

So I did what I had to do. Like the all round powerhouse of a woman I am.
And hired new gardeners.

I was so excited about them coming to sort it today that I'd planned a full afternoon in the garden with the boys.

Anyway, one of them has a bird who selfishly went into labour today so they cancelled.
I mean, yeah it's his first born. But Jesus. Look at my garden!

Fuck it, I'm going in.

I donned my camo gear, smeared war paint under my eyes and grabbed the rifle. I threw a jam sandwich at each of the kids and bid them farewell.

Because if you want anything doing, do it your fucking self.
(I'm definitely not doing it again though...)

***

This morning, Bill made Baby Tom some Weetabix whilst me and Our Lass were still in bed.
I'm not sure if this is promoting independence and evidence of his kind, caring nature towards his brother, or mum shaming.
Either way, he made less mess than his dad does but I've no milk left for my coffee.

***

Last night, Baby Tom took himself off to bed at 6pm. This morning, I found him sat downstairs <u>at 6am</u>, remote in hand, recording an episode of All Creatures Great and Small.

Pass the pipe and slippers!
They grow up so fast.

***

Kids are full blown into Harry Potter at the minute. As are me and Our Lass tbh…
So I obviously had to get them these.
Which they love.
They've been practicing spells since putting them on and it's adorable.

I asked them to raise their wands for a picture.
Spot the error.

***

Me: Bill, what are you doing?
Bill: I'm meditating.
Me: Oh right, very good.
Bill: It's what people can do when they're angry.
Bill to Thomas: Maybe Mummy could do with it to stop her from shouting?!

***

"Move the fucking plate."
Bill, aged 5 years and 353 days.

We almost made it to 6.

***

Our house has been so Harry Potter mad recently, that yesterday, Baby Tom saw a picture of Santa and said "Look Mummy, it's Dumbledore!"

***

Usually, for the kid's birthdays, I just put some snap out and invite the family round. Saves dealing with other people's children. Now Bill is of school age, and getting invites left, right and centre to parties, I thought it was time to bite the bullet and organise one. I've managed to avoid it for 5 years, I've not done bad.

I researched some venues and entertainers. Who mostly wanted half a years salary.
Fuck that. There's a pavilion round the corner, we'll do it ourselves.

We fed into the Harry Potter theme.
Created props, games, entertainment. It was actually pretty genius. Until the reality hit that we were the entertainment.
(Also, by 'we' I mean me and my mate. Daddy had nothing to do with it.)

Christ it was exhausting. And embarrassing. My own family and that of the other children sat watching as me and my pal ran around erratically attempting to control and engage 30 children.
Luckily we're creative geniuses and have a knack for demanding authority.
The best game we played as the entertainers was one we played in the kitchen called "Have a Glass of Wine Before the Next Ordeal."
That helped.

Anyway, somehow we pulled it off. Bill loved his party and apparently so did the other children (and some of the parents…). Of course I found the whole thing rather stressful and chaotic however on reflection, we did a fabulous job. Next year, I'll pay the half my salary for an entertainer.

And, as it was such a lovely, momentous occasion, we didn't take any pictures.

***

Becoming a parent has made me appreciate many things which I previously took for granted.

A lie in, obviously.
Being able to stay awake past <u>21:30</u>.
Eating a meal that no one is trying to steal.
Eating chocolate without hiding my head in a cupboard.
Actually, eating in general.
An uninterrupted bath.
An uninterrupted pee.
A trip to the shop - like when you just go, and it doesn't take 45 minutes to get out of the door.
Grandparents! The most wonderful babysitters! - I mean support system...

I'm particularly grateful this week, that despite my boys both having their birthday in the same month, there's a recycling bin collection in between them.

***

Daddy is on his Christmas do tonight.
I'm adult enough to admit there's some FOMO there but I went out last week so I can't really complain.

Anyway, he wanted a lift at the kids tea time so I decided, to cheer myself up a bit, and to save rushing around, we'd pick a KFC up on the way home.

As we dropped Daddy at his requested destination, Thomas shit himself.
A stench rivalling those his father creates yet more enduring as well, it was actual shit.

So now, as Our Lass skips merrily into the distance, to a world of beers, laughter and sequins, with not a child in sight, I'm sat in rush hour traffic, starving, whilst Bill gives me the 3rd degree over who's buried in the graves with the gravestones in the churchyard we just passed, which definitely is a church and not a synogogue because Daddy said so.
His attitude stinking as much as the faeces ridden atmosphere. And Thomas, crying because he's shit himself.

The KFC queue didn't smell as good as it usually does.
And when I finally got home to change him, it splashed on my face as I ripped open the sides too so the gravy didn't hit the spot like it usually does either...

***

When a ship is at the bottom of the ocean, it's call a ship wank.

Bill, aged 6.

***

So today we took the nappy off.
(Baby Tom, not me...)

I'm not ready. I don't want to. I remember HATING toilet training last time. But Daddy made me. Something to do with responsible parenting and not being neglectful blah blah blah.

10 pairs of pants, 3 sets of pj's, a pair of socks, 2 T-shirts, 4 carpet cleans, 3 sofa cleans and a full kitchen floor mop down later, Bill comes home from school that desperate for a wee he legs it to the toilet but unfortunately also has an accident, somehow managing to wet every item of clothing he was wearing including his coat.

So much for dry January.

I can feel myself falling deeper into that time of my cycle where I'm a complete psychotic arsehole and therefore decided to treat myself to a quick face mask in order to feed my absurdism.

Anyway, during application, Baby Tom, who has already had a momentous meltdown (obviously completely unrelated to mine…) decided it was time for his third breakfast.
I was rather swift in suppressing the urge to scream profanities in response to my offspring's request for food and decided that I'm probably a tad hangry too. Besides, a quick round of cheese on toast would pass the perfect amount of time until I needed to rinse my face.

Thomas needed the toilet 4 times before the toast had even popped. And didn't actually use it either time. Request number 5 was from me as he was dancing around with a worried look on his face, which he respectfully declined, by stamping his foot and screaming at me. He then ran upstairs, which I thought was odd. So I followed him only to find a trail of dribble patches leading straight to my darling son, stood atop of the stairs, pissing so strongly it actually created a solid stream through his clothes creating a river of hopelessness on the carpet.

Half a bottle of vanish, a piss covered cloth, a full change of clothes, a little cry and 2 rounds of burnt cheese on toast later, I was finally able to wash my face. My usual, and somewhat famous, zen like state finally restored.

If you too would like a collection of face masks for use in practicing self care over despair, let me know as they're on offer.
Head to my group or message me for details. I accept payments via bank transfer, PayPal and diazepam.

Buy two and be entered into a free draw to win a child!

***

In other news, Bill just called me Momma!
(I proceeded to ask him if he had in fact just called me such to which he responded, "Yes Debbie" but still, it's progress...)

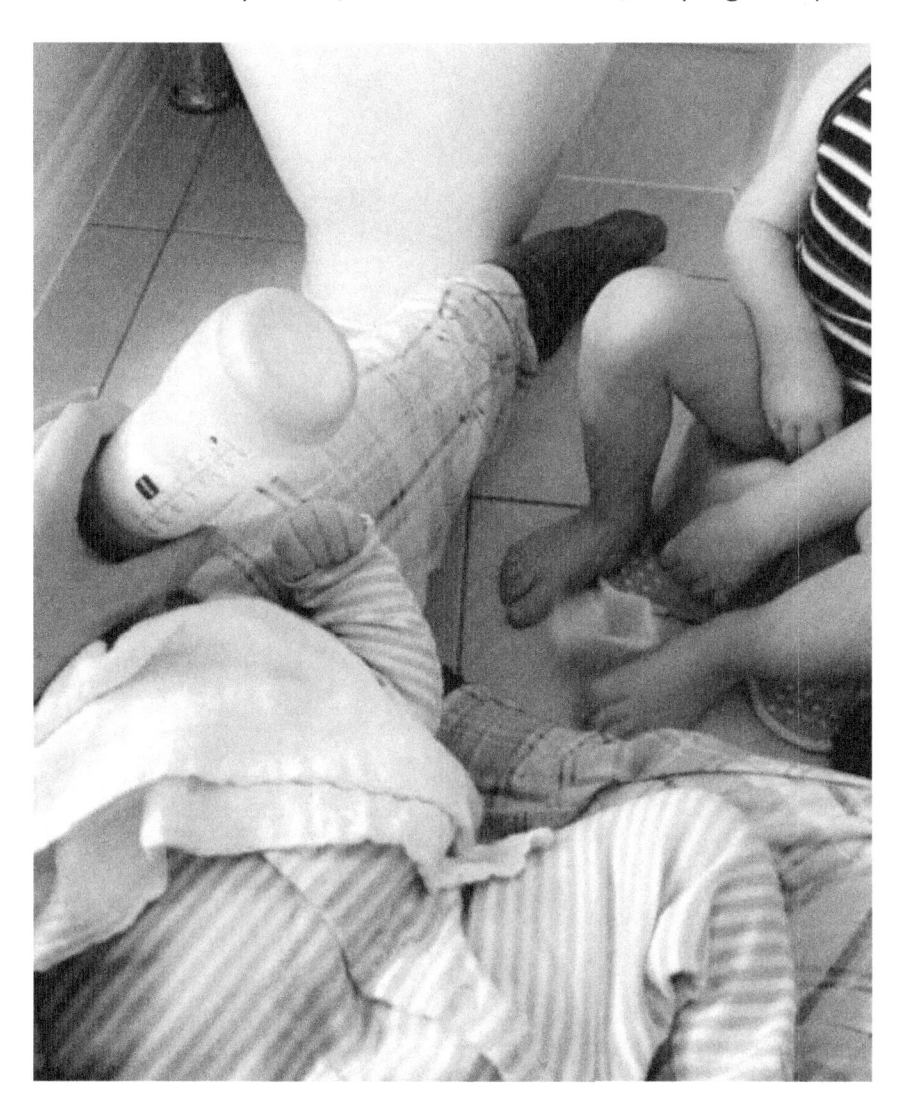

Printed in Great Britain
by Amazon